ARTIST TRANSCRIPTIONS
SAXOPHONE

John Coltrane Plays "Coltrane Changes"

T0045049

Contents

Transcribed by Masaya Yamaguchi

Cover photo: Raymond Ross

ISBN 0-634-03864-8

HAL•LEONARD® CORPORATION
7777 W. BLUEMOUND RD. P.O. BOX 13819 MILWAUKEE, WI 53213

Visit Hal Leonard Online at
www.halleonard.com

Special thanks to:

Dr. Todd Coolman

Jason Koransky & Dave Zaworski
(Down Beat)

Dr. Yusef Lateef

Prof. Henry Martin
(Chief Editor of *Annual Review of Jazz Studies*)

Jay Sweet

Extra special thanks to:

Dr. David Demsey

Dr. Lewis Porter
(Author of *John Coltrane: His Life and Music*)

Alice Coltrane

Ravi Coltrane

Foreword

COLTRANE CHANGES:
JOHN COLTRANE'S THIRDS CYCLE EXPLORATIONS

By David Demsey

The "Coltrane Changes" Concept

In the late 1950s, John Coltrane composed or arranged a series of tunes that used chord progressions based upon a series of key center movements by thirds, rather than the usual fourths and fifths of standard progressions. Its sound is so aurally identifiable and has received so much attention from jazz musicians that it has become known as "Coltrane changes." This progression is not only important because of its unique sound. Indeed, this chord sequence provided the harmonic impetus for the new level of harmonic freedom that Coltrane utilized for the rest of his career, influencing generations of musicians since the sixties. These thirds-based links between key centers are known as "third relationships," and occur frequently in all types of Western music. For example, some well-known standard tunes contain third relationships. "Autumn Leaves" has two main key centers, B-flat major and G minor, separated by a third. Since these two keys share the same key signature (they are the relative major and minor), they would be in a diatonic third relationship. Another standard, "In a Sentimental Mood," has an A section in the key of F major, and a bridge in the key of D-flat major. These two keys are separated by a major third, and have different key signatures. They form a chromatic third relationship.

Coltrane seized upon the concept of the chromatic third relationship, and created a "double" relationship where the progression moves to keys both a major third above and a major third below the "home" key (for example, as in the case of the first four measures of Coltrane's "Countdown," the keys of D, F-sharp, and B-flat major). In this unique relationship, not only are F-sharp and B-flat major each a major third away from the "home key" of D major, but they are also enharmonically a major third from each other. This cycle of three keys is symmetrical. In other words, each key is an equal distance of a major third from both of the others, providing the progression's unique and immediately identifiable sound.

Coltrane was familiar with this concept through several sources:

1. his musical relationship with Miles Davis for two periods (between September 1955 and April 1957, then again from early 1958 until April 1960) which involved nightly performances of Eddie Vinson's "Tune Up," which later became the model for "Countdown"

2. his tenure with Thelonious Monk in 1957, during which he explored unorthodox root motion and harmonic substitution

3. Coltrane's knowledge of the standard tune "Have You Met Miss Jones?", which includes a three-key thirds cycle in its bridge

4. his study of western European harmony with Dennis Sandole in Philadelphia in the early fifties, when he explored late 19th-century and early 20th-century harmonic techniques such as polytonality and 12-tone writing

5. Coltrane's study of the 1947 book *Thesaurus of Scale and Melodic Patterns* by Nicolas Slonimsky which contains numerous patterns used by Coltrane in his solos of this period, and most specifically contains the entire last half of "Giant Steps" (melody and chords) in its preface

Performance Notes

THIRDS CYCLES IN JOHN COLTRANE'S ARRANGEMENTS

"Body and Soul"

(Page 16)

"Body and Soul" was already established as a jazz classic via Coleman Hawkins' famous 1939 performance. Rather than merely imitate Hawkins' style, Coltrane took a distinctly different approach and made the tune his own. He transformed the tune by taking a brighter, "walking" tempo instead of a slow ballad feel, turning the A section into a mesmerizing modal vamp, and by reharmonizing the bridge with symmetrical thirds cycles. Instead of the usual ii-V-I in D major which normally occurs in measures 3 and 4 of the bridge, Coltrane inserts a thirds cycle. This progression starts on the tonic I chord, D major. Then, it moves quickly through a V-I progression in B-flat major, down a major third from D, then another V-I progression in F-sharp major, down another major third. Finally, it moves down another major third to return to the home key with a V-I in D major. Four measures later, this thirds cycle is repeated, this time down a step in the key of C major. It starts with the I chord, C major; then V-I down a major third in A-flat major; then down another major third in E major; then, finally down another major third to return to V-I in C major.

An additional note: the coda ending of Coltrane's "Body and Soul" contains another interesting thirds sound. After apparently ending the performance on the tonic chord of D♭maj7, the last four bars contain an Fmaj7 and Amaj7 (each moving up a major third) before a final cadence on D♭maj7.

"But Not for Me"

(Page 9)

Coltrane's version of George Gershwin's "But Not for Me" is perhaps the best known of his arrangements using thirds cycles; it is almost certainly the most widely heard. Although recorded only two days after "Body and Soul" in October 1960, it appeared on the popular *My Favorite Things* album, still one of the best-selling Coltrane recordings.

Coltrane reworked the harmony of the A sections to include two thirds cycles (the B sections are essentially identical to Gershwin's original). The harmony in the opening measures from Gershwin's original version is fairly static, using a simple cadential progression twice. He replaced these two phrases with a thirds cycle that employs V-I cadences in C-flat major and G-major, again each a major third away from the home key of E-flat major.

If measures 1-4 and measures 5-8 of "But Not for Me" have the same chord progression, why do they sound different, almost like the second four bars are a response to the first four? The answer is in the bass line, which does not take the traditional role of playing the roots of the harmony. Instead, it descends through the B-flat whole-tone scale in measures 1-4, then descends through the E-flat whole tone scale in the following four bars. Aside from implying a sort of V-I sound (B-flat moving to E-flat), it is also interesting to note that these two whole-tone scales make up all twelve pitches of the chromatic scale. This shows an example of Coltrane's experimentation with twelve-tone techniques, which he had been studying at the time, and which shows up with much more prominence in his tune "Miles Mode" and with great sophistication in his landmark "Giant Steps."

THIRDS CYCLES IN JOHN COLTRANE'S COMPOSITIONS

"Countdown"
(Page 19)

As far as any research detective work can determine, the earliest example of thirds cycles in Coltrane's music is his tune "Countdown," based upon the chord progression of Eddie Vinson's "Tune Up" which he had been playing every night with Miles Davis. The intensely packed form of "Countdown" contains thirds cycles in its first three four-bar phrases. In the opening of both "Tune Up" and "Countdown," the first phrase contains a simple ii-V-I progression in D major. In writing "Countdown," Coltrane inserted V-I progressions in the keys of B-flat major and F-sharp major between the ii chord (Em7) and the V7 chord (A7) in D major. In doing this, he puts the thirds cycle in actual use. The progression starts in D major, then moves down a major third to B-flat, down another major third to F-sharp, and finally down another major third to return to the home key of D major.

"26-2"
(Page 81)

The rather mystical-sounding title of "26-2" occurs for a more earthly reason: originally untitled, the tune was recorded on the 26th day of October, 1960, and it was the 2nd tune recorded. The tune is based upon a bebop anthem, Charlie Parker's "Confirmation." Coltrane plugs in the thirds cycle brilliantly here, keeping the original harmonic direction of the tune but making it very much his own. Parker's original A section started like a blues, with a cycle of fifths progression in F that ended on F7, then moving to the IV chord, B♭7. Coltrane replaces the cycle of fifths with his thirds cycle, moving from F to rapid V-I progressions in D-flat major (down a major third) and A major (down another major third), finally returning to F—but with a harmonic twist: instead of landing on F major as a tonic, he uses Cm7-F7 to move to the IV chord, exactly like Parker's original.

After arriving in B♭, Coltrane repeats the thirds cycle in that key: B♭ moves quickly through V-I in the key of G-flat and the key of D. There is another twist here, also, since the phrase needs to end in the original key of F: instead of ending the cycle on D major, he lands on Dm, then goes through a standard turnaround, Dm-G7-Gm-C7. The second A similarly moves to B♭ major in the fifth bar, but follows that with a thirds cycle in F to end the tune in the home key. The bridge of "26-2" follows "Confirmation" almost exactly, except for the first ii-V in B♭. Instead of the usual ii-V-I in B♭, Coltrane inserts a quick ii-V-I up a third in D major, then to V-I in B♭.

"Fifth House"
(Page 30)

Perhaps the most interesting tune of all of the standards-based thirds compositions is "Fifth House." The chord progression of this tune is based upon the standard tune "What Is This Thing Called Love?" The original A section contains a ii-V-i in F minor, and ii-V-I in C major. Instead of these cadences, Coltrane inserts thirds cycles in F and in C. There is an important and unique feature of this recorded performance, however: these chords are never actually played! There is only a tonic pedal (based around the pitches C and G) played throughout the A sections. Coltrane clearly implies these chords in his solo lines, but only the listener who has the sound of "Coltrane changes" firmly in mind will pick this up.

In the melody chorus, there are also no chords played, only the tonic pedal. The melody notes also imply these changes, but they also have the double implication of exotic scales, an F double harmonic minor (or phrygian harmonic minor) with a lowered second step and a raised seventh step, followed by the same scale in C.

OTHER COLTRANE ORIGINALS USING THIRDS CYCLES

"Central Park West"
(Page 18)

This beautiful tune is unique for two reasons:

1. It is the only example of a Coltrane ballad containing thirds cycles.

2. It is based around a symmetrical cycle of minor thirds involving four keys.

The tune is divided into two sections. The first section uses ii-V-I progressions in the major keys of B, D, F, and A-flat; the second section uses a B pedal over a shifting vamp. In the first section, not all of the key movements are by minor third; some are by tritone. In another reference to Coltrane's use of twelve-tone techniques, note that an inherent property of four equidistant ii-V-I cadences is that the combined roots of all twelve of the chords involved make up the twelve-pitch chromatic scale.

"Satellite"
(Page 74)

This 32-measure tune is based upon the classic standard "How High the Moon." As the original progression moves through the key areas of G major and F major, Coltrane replaces the cadences with thirds cycles in those keys, and uses a half-note-based melody similar to "Countdown." Note that the bass line uses the same descending whole-tone scale which appears in Coltrane's arrangement of "But Not for Me." There is also a partial thirds cycle near the end of the progression; cadences in E♭ major and G major move directly to the final D pedal. Note: this tune appears in several "underground" fake books under its original title, "Moon Man."

"Grand Central"
(Page 63)

This bebop-flavored tune from the *Cannonball Adderley and John Coltrane* album centers mostly around a descending series of ii-V's during its A section, and around a dominant pedal during its bridge. The last two bars of the bridge, however, use a partial thirds-cycle technique. The sequence of four dominant chords (B♭7 - E7 - A7 - C7) evokes a thirds sound, particularly since Coltrane's improvisation implies a D♭maj7 sound in place of the B♭7 chord.

"Exotica"
(Untitled Original) (Atlantic Version)
(Page 24)

This tune makes a consistent connection to Coltrane's arrangement of "Body and Soul." It has the same tempo and rhythm section groove, and its bridge is structured around the key centers of the classic ballad. The A sections of this AABAA tune open with, true to its title, a vamp based on an exotic scale form; the next four measures are a slightly altered version of a thirds cycle based on E, A-flat, and C.

THIRDS CYCLES IN
JOHN COLTRANE'S IMPROVISATIONS

John Coltrane did not use thirds-cycle techniques only in his compositions and arrangements. His use of superimposed thirds-cycle chord progressions during his improvised solos makes an important point: in Coltrane's thirds concept, he did not always require that the original changes be replaced by "Coltrane changes;" he also used them simultaneously with the original changes, "on the fly" during performances.

"Limehouse Blues"
(Page 66)

The best example of this is at the opening of his solo on "Limehouse Blues," which appeared on the album *Cannonball Adderley and John Coltrane*, actually recorded by Miles Davis' band without their leader, on a free day in Chicago in 1959. Coltrane begins his solo by improvising over the opening eight measures, containing four bars each of F7 and D7. Instead of playing over these changes as does the rhythm section, Coltrane superimposes a thirds cycle in B-flat over the F7 chord, and superimposes a thirds cycle in G over the D7 chord. The effect is head-spinning, and may have been the best possible response to Adderley's scorching alto solo which precedes his.

"Summertime"
(Page 86)

This mostly modal tune was a "sister arrangement" to Coltrane's immensely popular version of "My Favorite Things." The tunes were recorded three days apart in October 1960. At the end of Coltrane's first improvised chorus, while the rhythm section vamps on alternating Dm7 and B♭7 chords, Coltrane clearly outlines the first portion of a thirds cycle in D major. Inclusion of the final dominant seventh chord, A7, would have been premature, since the next chorus opens with an A augmented chord, so Coltrane dives down a half step lower to wait for the new chorus to begin.

"The Night Has a Thousand Eyes"
(Page 68)

This powerful arrangement revolves around a muscular dominant vamp leading into and ending the chord progression, which is performed in its original form. During Coltrane's improvised solo, however, he makes several references to thirds cycles. During each bridge of his three choruses, he implies two thirds cycles: a cycle in B-flat during the first four bars, and a cycle in A-flat during the next four measures. There are also more passing references to thirds-cycle sounds during the vamp sections in the second and third choruses. These measures do not clearly outline thirds changes, but imply portions of cycles.

About Masaya Yamaguchi and David Demsey

Masaya Yamaguchi

Guitarist Masaya Yamaguchi received an M.A. in Jazz Performance from the City College of New York. He is the project leader and transcriber of this book. He is also the author of *The Complete Thesaurus of Music Scale, Symmetrical Scales for Jazz Improvisation* (Masaya Music, 2006 Revised), *The Pentatonicism in Jazz: Creative Aspects and Practice* (Masaya Music, 2006 Revised), and of John Coltrane ("Multi-Tonic Changes") articles in *Down Beat* and *Annual Review of Jazz Studies 12*, 2003.

David Demsey

David Demsey, a saxophonist, is Professor of Music and Coordinator of Jazz Studies at William Paterson University. He is the author of *John Coltrane Plays "Giant Steps"* (Hal Leonard Corporation), and of John Coltrane articles which have appeared in *Down Beat* and *Annual Review of Jazz Studies*. His "Improvisation and Concepts of Virtuosity" is the final essay in the *Oxford Companion to Jazz*. He is a Contributing Editor for *Saxophone Journal* and *Jazz Player Magazine,* and has written liner notes for five Verve Records compact discs.

He has performed with the New York Philharmonic since 1995, including their 2000 Millennium European Tour and 1997 Latin American Tour, and is a member of the American Saxophone Quartet. He has appeared with such diverse artists as the trumpeter Clark Terry, bassists Milt Hinton and Rufus Reid, pianists Jim McNeely and James Williams, drummers Alan Dawson, Steve Smith, Horacee Arnold, and John Riley. He is a Selmer saxophone clinician, and has appeared at over 90 schools, colleges, and universities.

But Not for Me
Music and Lyrics by George Gershwin and Ira Gershwin

My Favorite Things / Atlantic 1361
Wednesday, October 26, 1960

BACK-CYCLING

Body and Soul

Words by Edward Heyman, Robert Sour and Frank Eyton
Music by John Green

Coltrane's Sound / Atlantic 1419
Monday, October 24, 1960

Central Park West

By John Coltrane

Coltrane's Sound / Atlantic 1419
Monday, October 24, 1960

Countdown
(Theme)
By John Coltrane

Giant Steps / Atlantic 1311
Monday, May 4, 1959

Countdown
By John Coltrane

Giant Steps / Atlantic 1311
Monday, May 4, 1959

Exotica (Untitled Original)

(Atlantic Version)

By John Coltrane

The Coltrane Legacy / Atlantic 1553
Monday, October 24, 1960

Exotica
(Roulette Version)
By John Coltrane

Like Sonny / Roulette CDP7939012
Recorded at United Recorders, Los Angeles
September 8, 1960

Fifth House
(Theme)
By John Coltrane

Coltrane Jazz / Atlantic 1354
Wednesday, December 2, 1959

Fifth House

By John Coltrane

Coltrane Jazz / Atlantic 1354
Wednesday, December 2, 1959

Giant Steps

By John Coltrane

Giant Steps / Atlantic 1311
Tuesday, May 5, 1959

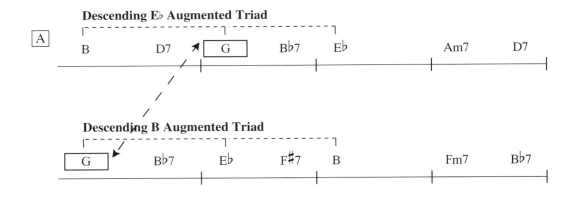

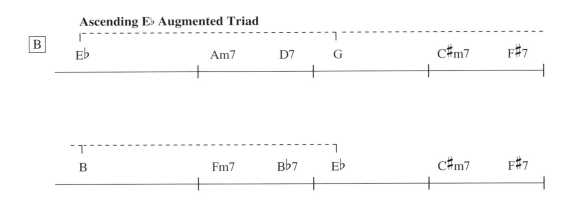

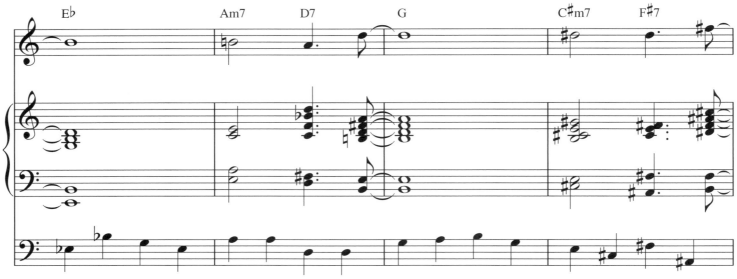

④ CD Time 0:40

44

Grand Central

(Theme)

By John Coltrane

The Cannonball Adderly Quintet in Chicago
**Mercury (MG 20449) / February 3, 1959,
at Universal Recording Studios, Chicago**

Grand Central

By John Coltrane

The Cannonball Adderly Quintet in Chicago
**Mercury (MG 20449) / February 3, 1959,
at Universal Recording Studios, Chicago**

Limehouse Blues

Words by Douglas Furber
Music by Philip Braham

The Cannonball Adderly Quintet in Chicago
**Mercury (MG 20449) / February 3, 1959,
at Universal Recording Studios, Chicago**

The Night Has a Thousand Eyes

Theme from the Paramount Picture *THE NIGHT HAS A THOUSAND EYES*

Words by Buddy Bernier
Music by Jerry Brainin

Coltrane's Sound / Atlantic 1419
Wednesday, October 26, 1960

Satellite
(Theme)
By John Coltrane

Coltrane's Sound / Atlantic 1419
Monday, October 24, 1960

Satellite
By John Coltrane

Coltrane's Sound / Atlantic 1419
Monday, October 24, 1960

④ CD Time 2:18

26-2

(Theme)
By John Coltrane

The Coltrane Legacy / Atlantic 1970
Wednesday, October 26, 1960

26-2

By John Coltrane

The Coltrane Legacy / Atlantic 1970
Wednesday, October 26, 1960

Summertime
from *Porgy and Bess* ®
By George Gershwin, Du Bose and Dorothy Heyward and Ira Gershwin

My Favorite Things / Atlantic 1361
Monday, October 24, 1960

ARTIST TRANSCRIPTIONS

Artist Transcriptions are authentic, note-for-note transcriptions of the hottest artists in jazz, pop, and rock today. These outstanding, accurate arrangements are in an easy-to-read format which includes all essential lines. Artist Transcriptions can be used to perform, sequence or reference.

GUITAR & BASS

The Guitar Style of George Benson
00660113 .... $14.95

The Guitar Book of Pierre Bensusan
00699072 .... $19.95

Ron Carter – Acoustic Bass
00672331 .... $16.95

Charley Christian – The Art of Jazz Guitar
00026704 .... $9.95

Stanley Clarke Collection
00672307 .... $19.95

Al Di Meola – Cielo E Terra
00604041 .... $14.95

Al Di Meola – Friday Night in San Francisco
00660115 .... $14.95

Al Di Meola – Music, Words, Pictures
00604043 .... $14.95

Kevin Eubanks Guitar Collection
00672319 .... $19.95

The Jazz Style of Tal Farlow
00673245 .... $19.95

Bela Fleck and the Flecktones
00672359 Melody/Lyrics/Chords $18.95

David Friesen – Years Through Time
00673253 .... $14.95

Best of Frank Gambale
00672336 .... $22.95

Jim Hall – Jazz Guitar Environments
00699389 Book/CD $19.95

Jim Hall – Exploring Jazz Guitar
00699306 .... $17.95

Scott Henderson Guitar Book
00699330 .... $19.95

Allan Holdsworth –
Reaching for the Uncommon Chord
00604049 .... $14.95

Leo Kottke – Eight Songs
00699215 .... $14.95

Wes Montgomery – Guitar Transcriptions
00675536 .... $17.95

Joe Pass Collection
00672353 .... $18.95

John Patitucci
00673216 .... $14.95

Django Reinhardt Anthology
00027083 .... $14.95

The Genius of Django Reinhardt
00026711 .... $10.95

Django Reinhardt – A Treasury of Songs
00026715 .... $12.95

Great Rockabilly Guitar Solos
00692820 .... $14.95

Johnny Smith Guitar Solos
00672374 .... $16.95

Mike Stern Guitar Book
00673224 .... $16.95

Mark Whitfield
00672320 .... $19.95

Jack Wilkins – Windows
00673249 .... $14.95

Gary Willis Collection
00672337 .... $19.95

CLARINET

Buddy De Franco Collection
00672423 .... $19.95

TROMBONE

J.J. Johnson Collection
00672332 .... $19.95

TRUMPET

The Chet Baker Collection
00672435 .... $19.95

Randy Brecker
00673234 .... $17.95

The Brecker Brothers...
And All Their Jazz
00672351 .... $19.95

Best of the Brecker Brothers
00672447 .... $19.95

Miles Davis – Originals Volume 1
00672448 .... $19.95

Miles Davis – Originals Volume 2
00672451 .... $19.95

FLUTE

Eric Dolphy Collection
00672379 .... $19.95

James Newton – Improvising Flute
00660108 .... $14.95

The Lew Tabackin Collection
00672455 .... $19.95

Miles Davis – Standards Vol. 1
00672450 .... $19.95

Miles Davis – Standards Vol. 2
00672449 .... $19.95

The Dizzy Gillespie Collection
00672479 .... $19.95

Freddie Hubbard
00673214 .... $14.95

Tom Harrell Jazz Trumpet
00672382 .... $19.95

Jazz Trumpet Solos
00672363 .... $9.95

PIANO & KEYBOARD

Monty Alexander Collection
00672338 .... $19.95

Monty Alexander Plays Standards
00672487 .... $19.95

Kenny Barron Collection
00672318 .... $22.95

Warren Bernhardt Collection
00672364 .... $19.95

Cyrus Chesnut Collection
00672439 .... $19.95

Billy Childs Collection
00673242 .... $19.95

Chick Corea – Elektric Band
00603126 .... $15.95

Chick Corea – Paint the World
00672300 .... $12.95

Bill Evans Collection
00672365 .... $19.95

Bill Evans – Piano Interpretations
00672425 .... $19.95

The Benny Goodman Collection
00672492 .... $14.95

Benny Green Collection
00672329 .... $19.95

Vince Guaraldi Jazz Transcriptions
00672486 .... $19.95

Herbie Hancock Collection
00672419 .... $19.95

Gene Harris Collection
00672446 .... $19.95

Hampton Hawes
00672438 .... $19.95

Ahmad Jamal Collection
00672322 .... $22.95

Jazz Master Classics for Piano
00672354 .... $14.95

Brad Mehldau Collection
00672476 .... $19.95

Thelonious Monk Plays Jazz Standards – Volume 1
00672390 .... $19.95

Thelonious Monk Plays Jazz Standards – Volume 2
00672391 .... $19.95

Thelonious Monk – Intermediate
Piano Solos
00672392 .... $14.95

Jelly Roll Morton – The Piano Rolls
00672433 .... $12.95

Michel Petrucciani
00673226 .... $17.95

Bud Powell Classics
00672371 .... $19.95

Bud Powell Collection
00672376 .... $19.95

André Previn Collection
00672437 .... $19.95

Horace Silver Collection
00672303 .... $19.95

Art Tatum Collection
00672316 .... $22.95

Art Tatum Solo Book
00672355 .... $19.95

Billy Taylor Collection
00672357 .... $24.95

McCoy Tyner
00673215 .... $16.95

Cedar Walton Collection
00672321 .... $19.95

The Teddy Wilson Collection
00672434 .... $19.95

SAXOPHONE

Julian "Cannonball" Adderly Collection
00673244 .... $19.95

Michael Brecker
00673237 .... $19.95

Michael Brecker Collection
00672429 .... $19.95

The Brecker Brothers...
And All Their Jazz
00672351 .... $19.95

Best of the Brecker Brothers
00672447 .... $19.95

Benny Carter Plays Standards
00672315 .... $22.95

Benny Carter Collection
00672314 .... $22.95

James Carter Collection
00672394 .... $19.95

John Coltrane – Giant Steps
00672349 .... $19.95

John Coltrane – A Love Supreme
00672494 .... $12.95

John Coltrane Plays "Coltrane Changes"
00672493 .... $19.95

Coltrane Plays Standards
00672453 .... $19.95

John Coltrane Solos
00673233 .... $22.95

Paul Desmond Collection
00672328 .... $19.95

Paul Desmond – Standard Time
00672454 .... $19.95

Stan Getz
00699375 .... $18.95

Stan Getz – Bossa Novas
00672377 .... $19.95

Stan Getz – Standards
00672375 .... $17.95

Great Tenor Sax Solos
00673254 .... $18.95

Joe Henderson – Selections from
"Lush Life" & "So Near So Far"
00673252 .... $19.95

Best of Joe Henderson
00672330 .... $22.95

Jazz Master Classics for Tenor Sax
00672350 .... $18.95

Best of Kenny G
00673239 .... $19.95

Kenny G – Breathless
00673229 .... $19.95

Kenny G – Classics in the Key of G
00672462 .... $19.95

Kenny G – Faith: A Holiday Album
00672485 .... $14.95

Kenny G – The Moment
00672373 .... $19.95

Joe Lovano Collection
00672326 .... $19.95

James Moody Collection – Sax and Flute
00672372 .... $19.95

The Frank Morgan Collection
00672416 .... $19.95

The Art Pepper Collection
00672301 .... $19.95

Sonny Rollins Collection
00672444 .... $19.95

David Sanborn Collection
00675000 .... $16.95

The Lew Tabackin Collection
00672455 .... $19.95

Stanley Turrentine Collection
00672334 .... $19.95

Ernie Watts Saxophone Collection
00673256 .... $18.95

FOR MORE INFORMATION, SEE YOUR LOCAL MUSIC DEALER,
OR WRITE TO:

HAL•LEONARD® CORPORATION

7777 W. BLUEMOUND RD. P.O. BOX 13819 MILWAUKEE, WI 53213

Visit our web site for a complete listing of our titles with songlists.
www.halleonard.com

Prices and availability subject to change without notice.
Some products may not be available outside the U.S.A.